# HAL LEONARD

# TENOR BANJO METHOD

### BY FRED SOKOLOW

**PLAYBACK+**
Speed • Pitch • Balance • Loop

To access audio visit:
**www.halleonard.com/mylibrary**

Enter Code
5410-5428-0054-8488

## The Recording

Tenor banjo, other stringed instruments, and vocals: Fred Sokolow
Sound engineer: Michael Monagan
Recorded at Sossity Sound

Editorial assistance by Ronny S. Schiff

Cover and interior photos of Sierra model tenor banjo
courtesy of Deering Banjo Company. Photos by Chris Bryan.

ISBN: 978-1-5400-0120-7

Visit Hal Leonard Online at
**www.halleonard.com**

Contact Us:
**Hal Leonard**
7777 West Bluemound Road
Milwaukee, WI 53213
Email: info@halleonard.com

In Europe contact:
**Hal Leonard Europe Limited**
42 Wigmore Street
Marylebone, London, W1U 2RN
Email: info@halleonardeurope.com

In Australia contact:
**Hal Leonard Australia Pty. Ltd.**
4 Lentara Court
Cheltenham, Victoria, 3192 Australia
Email: info@halleonard.com.au

# CONTENTS

# TRACK LIST/SONG INDEX

# INTRODUCTION

The four-string tenor banjo is heard mostly in Dixieland bands, strumming chords and soloing in a chordal style. But tenor banjo, strumming four beats to the bar, was the driving rhythmic force in the jazz and swing bands of the teens and 1920s, when a dance craze swept the U.S. So it's not unusual to see a tenor banjo in the retro-swing bands, large and small, that are keeping music from the 1920s and 1930s alive today. You'll also hear tenor banjoists in Irish bands picking out the melodies of jigs and reels, often in unison with a fiddle or other melodic instrument.

Even though it's associated with Dixieland, retro swing, and Irish music, the tenor banjo, like all fretted instruments, can play the music of practically any genre. Once you've learned the basics, as taught in this book, you can strum or pick along with a country, blues, punk, or rock ensemble. And as a soloist (without any accompanying instruments), you can play a Beatles tune, a classical piece, or anything else that involves chords and melody.

This book, along with the accompanying sound files, teaches the basic chords and scales needed to strum backup and to improvise solos. If you like the sound of the banjo—and nothing sounds like a banjo except a banjo!—you'll enjoy the tunes and exercises in these pages.

Good luck!

*Fred Sokolow*

Fred Sokolow

P.S. In case anyone asks, the tenor banjo evolved from the five-string banjo, which originated in Africa. The first tenor banjos, called "tango banjos," were made around 1910, when Argentinian tango music and tango bands were popular in the U.S. By 1920, the tenor banjo was an essential instrument in the dance bands that played early jazz and swing. It was loud, which was important in an era of no amplification, and it provided a steady rhythm that dancers needed. It was also tuned in 5ths, so violin and mandolin players could easily adapt to it. Hopefully, you can adapt to it too!

# PARTS OF THE BANJO

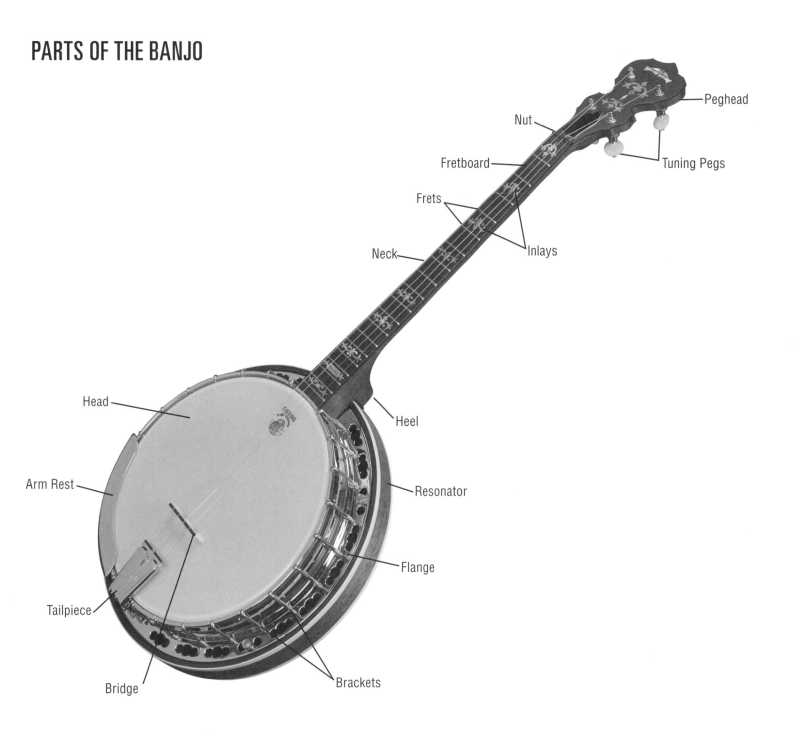

- The *resonator* is optional; some tenor banjos are open-backed. A resonator makes the instrument louder and pushes the sound forward toward a microphone or an audience.

- The *inlays* are fret markings that help you navigate the fretboard. They are usually located at the fifth, seventh, 10th, and 12th frets (and in many more places on some banjos).

- The *head*, like a drumhead, was traditionally made of hide. Plastic heads have been much more common since about 1960. They sound brighter and are less subject to changing with the weather.

- The *bridge* is not attached to the head; the string tension alone holds it in place. When you remove the strings, the bridge comes off.

- *Brackets* allow you to tighten or loosen the head. A tighter head sounds brighter. The head is tight enough when the bridge doesn't cause a depression in it. If your banjo has a resonator, it must be removed to access the brackets. You also need a banjo wrench that matches the size of your banjo's brackets.

# TUNING

The standard tenor banjo is tuned in 5ths—from low to high (string 4 to string 1): C–G–D–A. This is similar to the mandolin and violin, which are also tuned in 5ths, but the tenor banjo sounds a 4th (five frets) higher.

If there's no electronic tuner handy, get a C note from a tuning fork, pitch pipe, piano, or some other instrument that you know is in proper tune, and use the time-honored string-to-string method to tune:

- Tune the open C, fourth string to a tuning fork, piano, or other pitch source.

- Fret the C string at the seventh fret. Match the open G, third string to this note.

- Fret the G string at the seventh fret. Match the open D, second string to this note.

- Fret the D string at the seventh fret. Match the open A, first string to this note.

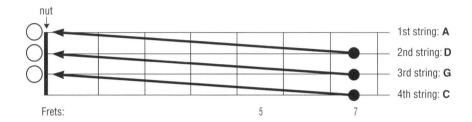

Or you can use the tuning notes on this handy audio track!

**Tuning Notes**

TRACK 1

# NOTES ON THE BANJO

You don't have to memorize all the notes on the fretboard at this point, but for reference, here they are:

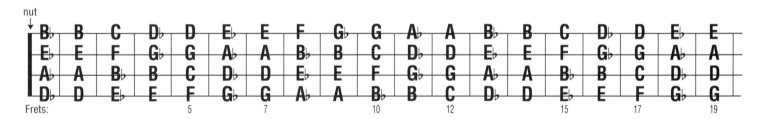

# HOLDING THE PICK

Most tenor banjo players use a plastic pick and hold it as shown in the image below.

# PLAYING POSITION

Even if you come from Alabama, you don't really hold a banjo on your knee! You hold it on your right thigh or in your lap as shown below.

The wrist of your fretting hand should be fairly straight, and there should be a space between your palm and the banjo neck.

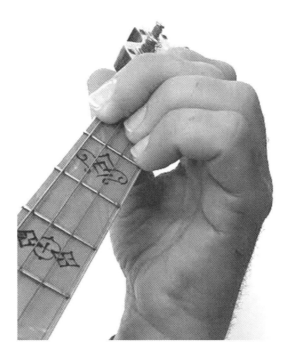

# ACCOMPANIMENT

Though the tenor banjo can be fingerpicked, most players strum with a pick. Play the C chord shown here and practice the following strumming and picking patterns:

- The numbers below the chord grid indicate which fret-hand fingers to use: 1 = index finger, 2 = middle finger, 3 = ring finger, 4 = little finger.

- Fret the strings with the tips of your fingers near (but not touching) the fret wire. Keep your fingernails short!

## FOUR BEATS TO THE BAR

This simple shuffle beat strum consists of four downstrokes:

TRACK 2

A slight rhythmic change turns the same pattern into a straight-eighths rock beat. Notice the accent marks (>) indicating that you should strum a little louder.

## DAMPING

A variation of the four-beats-to-the-bar strum involves *damping*. Stopping every other chord's sustain creates a swing rhythm. You damp strings by lifting your fretting fingers so that they're still touching the strings but not pressing them down to the fretboard. In the case of open chords, which contain open strings as well as fretted notes, you'll need to stop the open strings with either your pick hand or another free fret-hand finger. In the music, *staccato* markings (dots above or below a note) indicate the damped chords:

TRACK 3

## ANOTHER VARIATION

Add upstrokes for a busier shuffle beat:

TRACK 4

# A COUNTRY STRUM

Picking single, lower strings creates a country feel in 2/4 or 3/4 time:

TRACK 5

# FINGERPICKING

You can create countless fingerpicking patterns for variety. And even though we use the term *fingerpicking*, you could also play these arpeggio patterns with a pick if you'd like.

TRACK 6

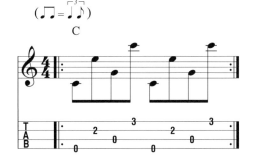
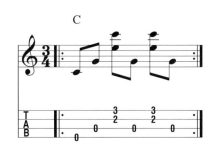

# THE NUMBER SYSTEM

Before you start learning chords, a little music theory will help make some sense of the tunes and exercises up ahead.

Often, musicians use numbers, instead of letters, to identify chords. You frequently hear things such as, "Go to the 4 chord," or "Go to the 2 minor." The numbers refer to notes of the major scale. Since C is the first note in the C major scale (C–D–E–F–G–A–B), a C chord is the 1 chord in the key of C. D, D7 (D dominant seventh), or Dm (D minor) is the 2 chord, and E, E7, or Em is the 3 chord, etc. In the key of D major (D–E–F#–G–A–B–C#), E (or E7 or Em) is the 2 chord. In the number system, a minor chord is represented with a dash after it. Therefore, a Dm chord in the key of C would be shown as "2-" in a chart.

No matter which key you're in, moving from the 1 chord to the 5 chord has a certain sound. So does going from 1 to 4. It's the spaces between chords—the *intervals*—that give a chord progression its unique sound. Once you can recognize the sounds of the various intervals, such as 1–4 or 1–5, you begin to understand how music works, and you'll eventually be able to play a song in any key. You're not just memorizing letter names; you're internalizing the song's structure.

# THE 1-4-5 CHORD FAMILY

Regardless of a song's key, the 1, 4, and 5 chords are the "usual suspects"—the chords that are most likely to occur. Millions of folk, country, blues, bluegrass, and classic rock songs consist of just those three chords. They can appear in any order imaginable. It's helpful to have the chord families memorized for various keys. The 1, 4, and 5 chords in the key of C, for example, are C, F, and G.

"When the Saints Go Marching In" is an essential tune for Dixieland bands, and it's often played to close a show. It only has three chords: 1, 4, and 5. In the key of C, that's C, F, and G (or G7). The strum heard on the recording is like the one played in track 3. Here are the F, G, and G7 chords:

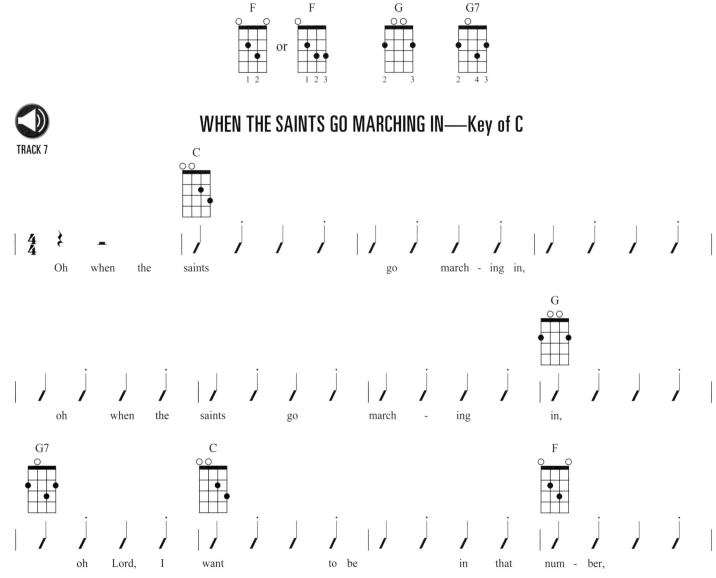

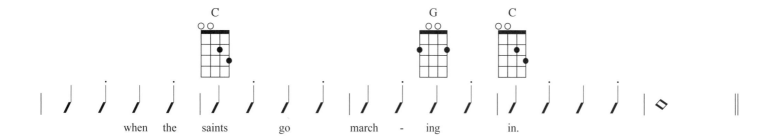

when the saints go march - ing in.

If this 1869 drinking song, "Little Brown Jug," sounds familiar, it's because Dave Bartholomew borrowed the melody when he wrote "My Ding-A-Ling," which became a #1 hit for Chuck Berry in 1972. It can be played with three chords: 1, 4, and 5 in the key of F (F, B♭, and C or C7). The strum used here is the same as on track 4. Here are your new chords:

## LITTLE BROWN JUG—Key of F

**TRACK 8**

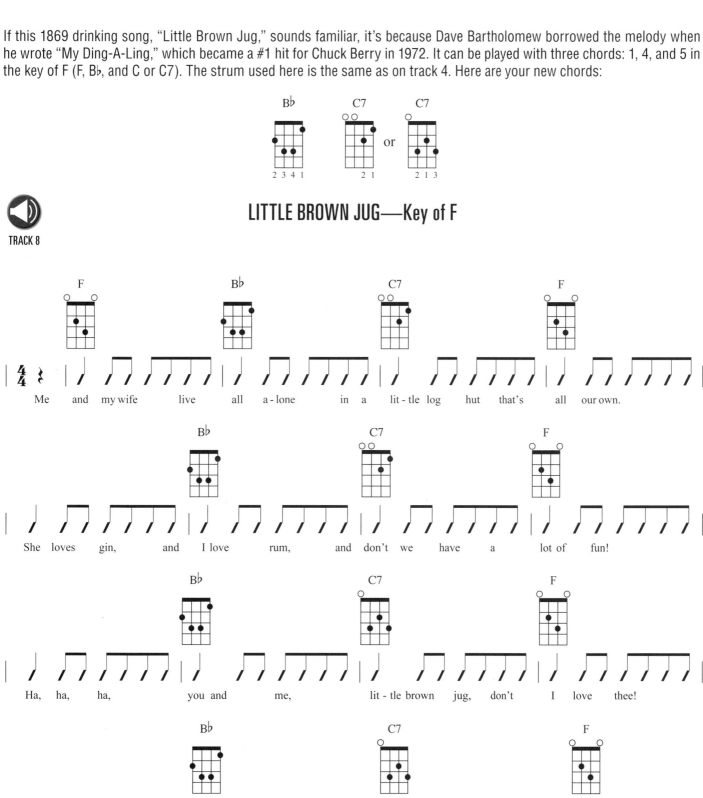

Me and my wife live all a - lone in a lit - tle log hut that's all our own.

She loves gin, and I love rum, and don't we have a lot of fun!

Ha, ha, ha, you and me, lit - tle brown jug, don't I love thee!

Ha, ha, ha, you and me, lit - tle brown jug, don't I love thee!

Words and Music by Joseph E. Winner
Copyright © 2019 by HAL LEONARD LLC
International Copyright Secured   All Rights Reserved

This folk blues, originally called "Frankie and Albert," describes a real incident—a murder that took place in 1899 in St. Louis. It uses the 1, 4, and 5 chords in the key of G: G, C, and D (or D7). The strum heard on the recording is the same as in track 5.

Below are your new chords, D and D7. Notice the curved line appearing over the dots in these chords. These are called *barres*, which tell you to fret more than one string at a time with only one finger. In this case, lay your index finger flat across the indicated strings so you're fretting two notes with that one finger:

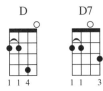

TRACK 9

## FRANKIE AND JOHNNY—Key of G

Anonymous Blues Ballad
Copyright © 2019 by HAL LEONARD LLC
International Copyright Secured   All Rights Reserved

A very popular Dixieland standard from 1902, "Bill Bailey" makes use of the 1, 4, and 5 chords in the key of B♭ (B♭, E♭, and F or F7) as well as B♭7, E♭m, G7, and C7. You'll hear the strum from track 4 on the recording. Here are the new chords:

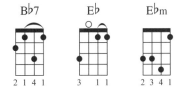

**TRACK 10**

## BILL BAILEY, WON'T YOU PLEASE COME HOME—Key of B♭

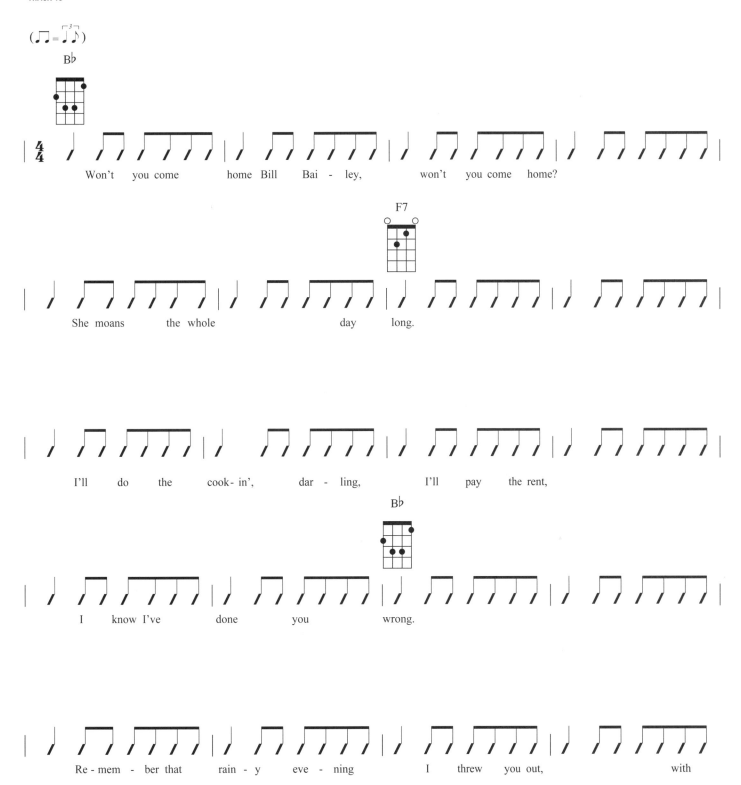

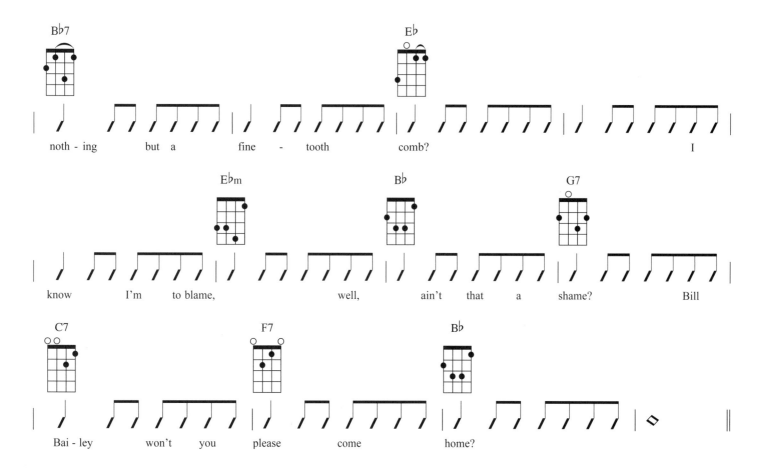

noth - ing    but a    fine - tooth    comb?                              I

know    I'm    to blame,              well,    ain't    that a    shame?              Bill

Bai - ley    won't    you    please    come    home?

Because of the repeated lyric, "I ain't gonna study war no more," "Down by the Riverside" has been sung by anti-war activists in recent history, but it's a 150-year-old African-American spiritual. To play it in the key of D, you'll need the 1, 4, and 5 (D, G, and A or A7) chords as well as D7. The strum from track 3 is used on the recording. Here are the A and A7 chords:

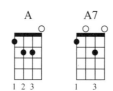

TRACK 11

# DOWN BY THE RIVERSIDE—Key of D

**Shuffle feel**

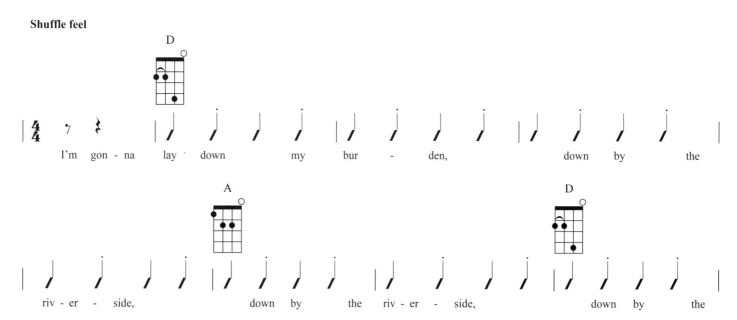

I'm gon - na    lay    down    my    bur - den,              down    by    the

riv - er - side,              down    by    the    riv - er - side,              down    by    the

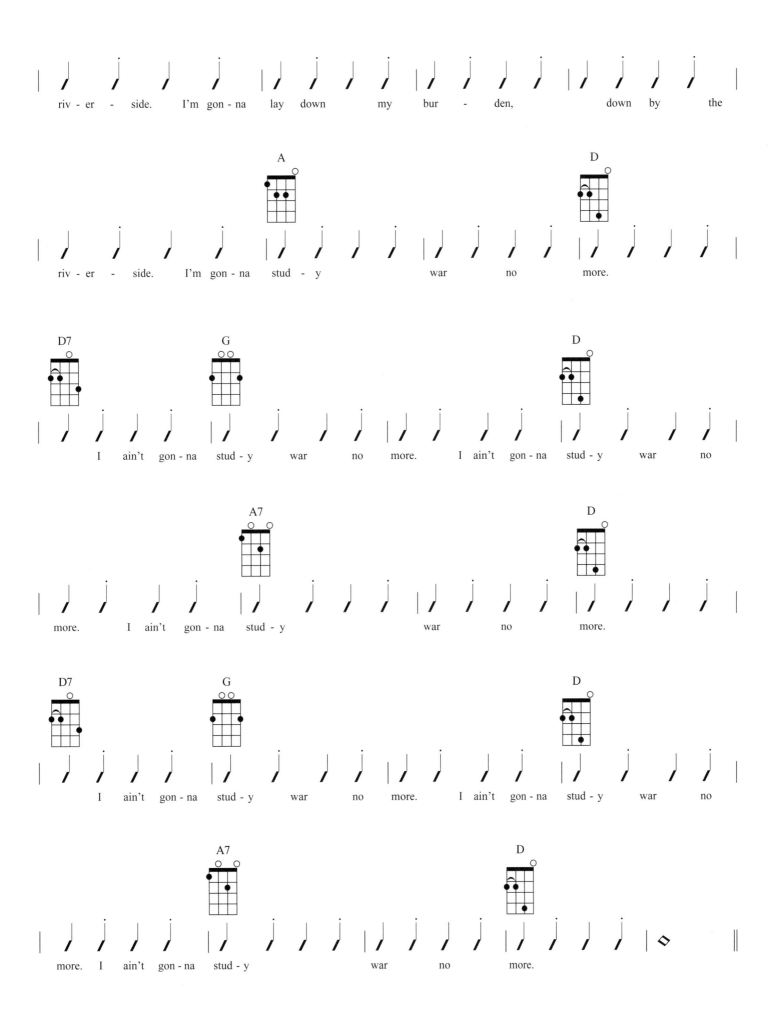

W. C. Handy wrote this paean to the famous street in Memphis in 1916, and its success jump-started his career. There are three sections to the tune. This third section in the key of A uses the 1, 4, and 5 chords (A, D, and E7) as well as A7 and D7. (Many blues tunes make liberal use of seventh chords in this way.) The first picking pattern in track 6 is heard on the recording. Here are the new chords (E and E7):

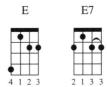

**TRACK 12**

# BEALE STREET BLUES—Key of A

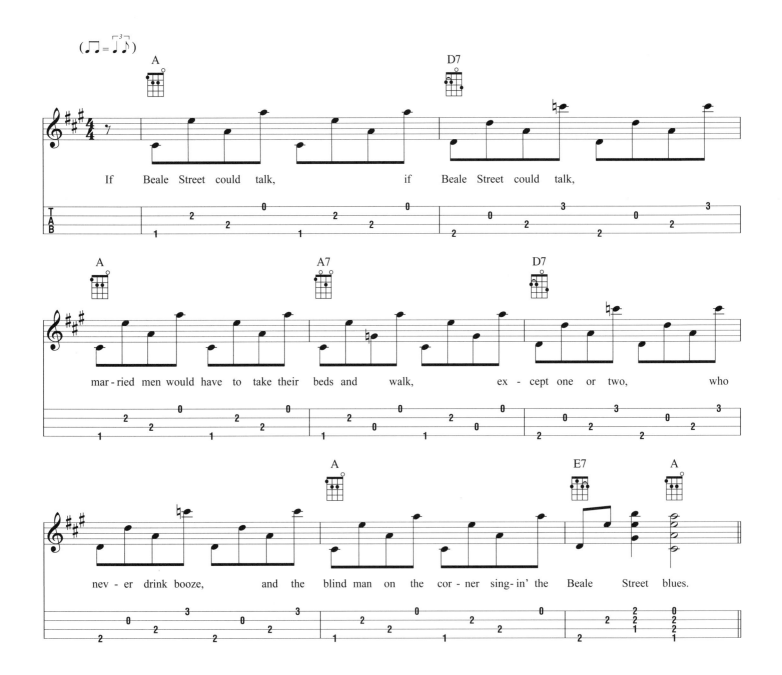

Buddy Bolden and other early New Orleans jazz pioneers played this folk blues, and it has since been recorded by jazz, blues, folk, rock, and R&B artists. This version is in the key of E and uses the 1, 4, and 5 chords—all of which appear as major chords and dominant sevenths. The second picking pattern in track 5 is used on the following song. Here are the new chords:

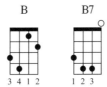

## CARELESS LOVE—Key of E

TRACK 13

# RELATIVE MINORS

Every major chord has a *relative minor*—a closely related chord that is an interval of a 6th higher. For example, to find the relative minor of the C major chord, count to the sixth note of the C major scale. A is the sixth note, so A minor is the relative minor of C major.

If a tune has more than just the immediate chord family (1, 4, and 5), the next chords most likely to occur are the relative minors of the 1, 4, and 5 chords. In the key of C, for example, C, F, and G are the immediate chord family. Their relative minors—Am, Dm, and Em, respectively—make an extended chord family. A song in the key of C is likely to include any one, two, or all three of these minor chords.

Here are some minor chord shapes and a few tunes that make use of them:

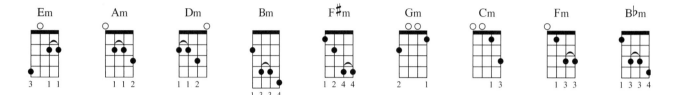

Originally a hit in 1919, this uptempo number had a comeback in the 1950s when novelty songster Spike Jones recorded it. Jim Kweskin & the Jug Band brought it a new audience in the early 1960s. The recording uses the strum pattern from track 4.

**TRACK 14**

## BLUES MY NAUGHTY SWEETIE GAVE TO ME—Key of D Minor

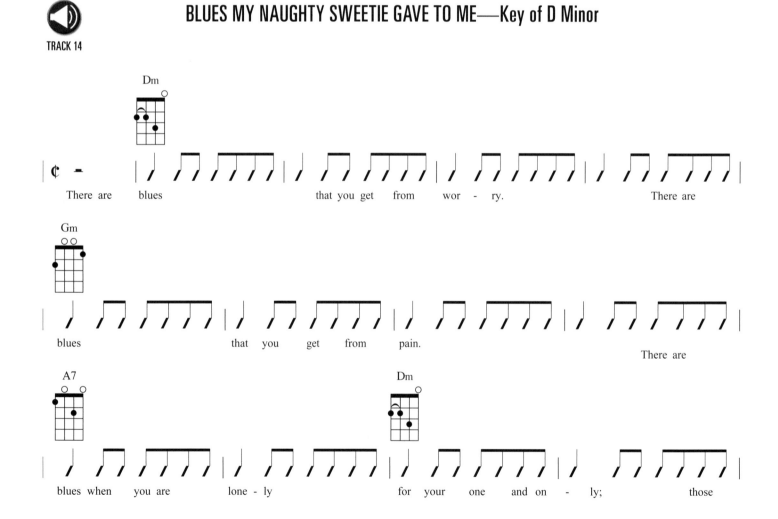

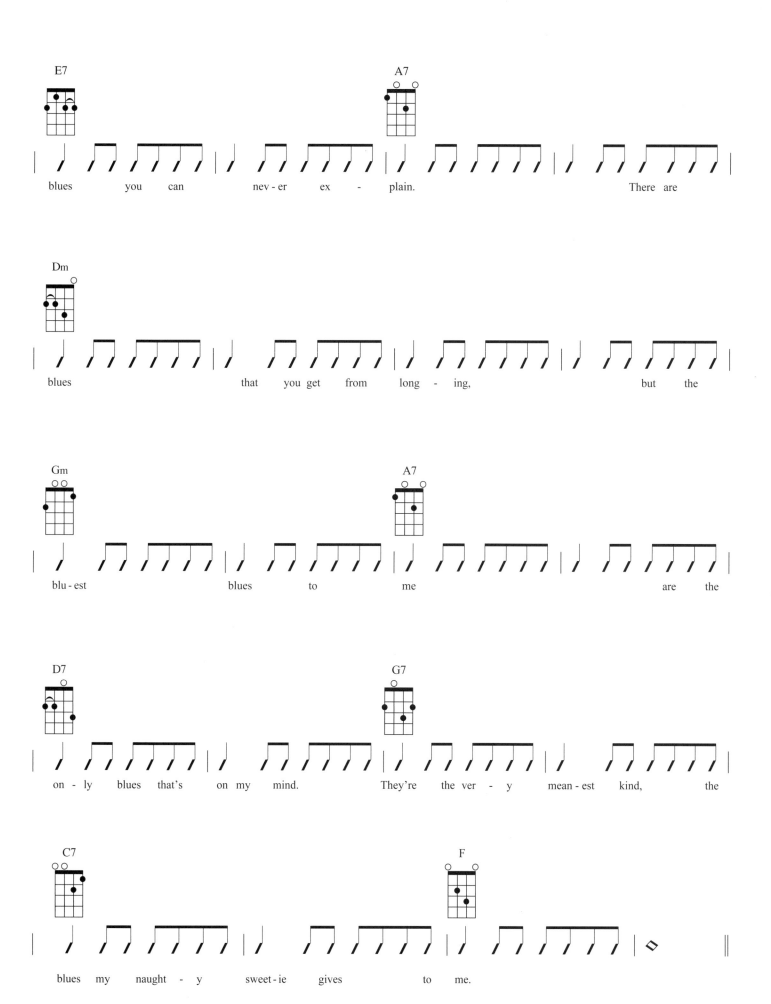

E7

blues    you   can    nev - er   ex  -   plain.                    There   are

Dm

blues              that   you  get   from   long - ing,                    but   the

Gm                                          A7

blu - est              blues   to   me                              are   the

D7                                          G7

on - ly   blues   that's    on   my   mind.    They're   the   ver - y   mean - est   kind,   the

C7                                          F

blues   my   naught - y    sweet - ie   gives              to   me.

Here's another tune that looms large in the Dixieland and early jazz repertoire. There are notable recordings by countless singers and instrumentalists, from Louis Armstrong to Rickie Lee Jones to Betty Boop. The strumming combines the patterns used on tracks 3 and 4.

TRACK 15

## SAINT JAMES INFIRMARY—Key of A Minor

Words and Music by Joe Primrose
Copyright © 2019 by HAL LEONARD LLC
International Copyright Secured   All Rights Reserved

# THREE MOVEABLE MAJOR CHORDS

Moveable chords have no open strings, so they can be played all over the fretboard. For example, here are three moveable major chords played in different places on the fretboard. The *root* of each chord shape (the note that gives the chord its name) is circled.

They are the D, G, and A formations:

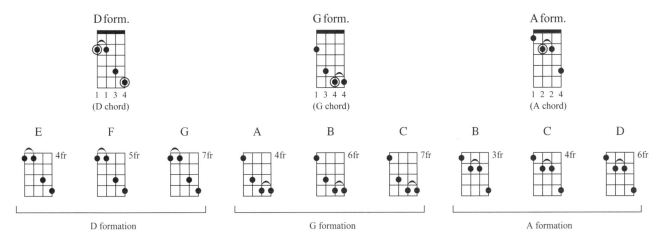

## Major Chord Families

Practice playing these chords in their *chord families*. The chord relationships in the three chord families below are moveable. For example, when the D formation is the 1 chord, the A formation one fret lower is the 5 chord.

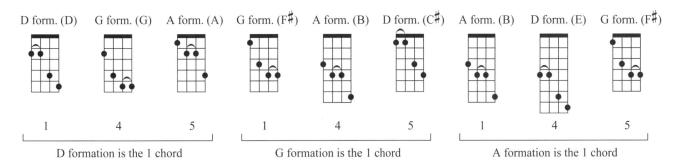

The following three exercises have the same chord progression as "Little Brown Jug": 1–4–5–1. Play each one in several places on the fretboard to get familiar with the three chord families.

TRACK 16

## LITTLE BROWN JUG—With Moveable Chords

### D Formation Chord Family

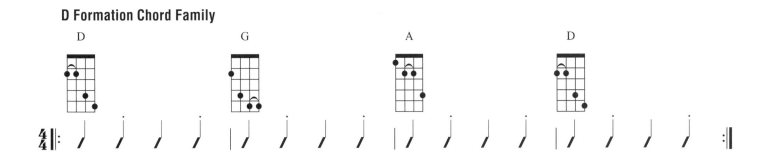

**G Formation Chord Family**

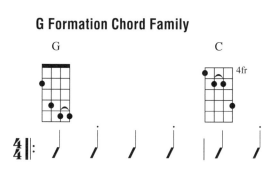

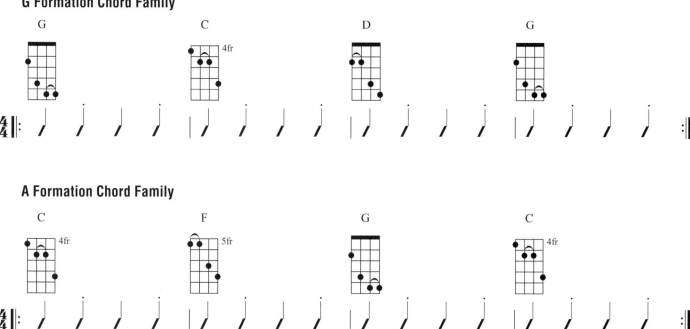

**A Formation Chord Family**

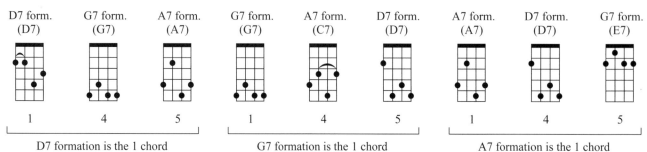

# THREE MOVEABLE SEVENTH CHORDS

The three moveable major chord formations can be altered to create seventh chords. Here they are:

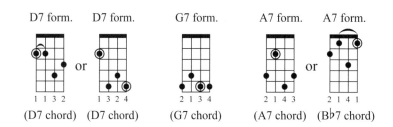

**Seventh Chord Families**

And here are the moveable seventh chord families:

| D7 form.<br>(D7) | G7 form.<br>(G7) | A7 form.<br>(A7) | G7 form.<br>(G7) | A7 form.<br>(C7) | D7 form.<br>(D7) | A7 form.<br>(A7) | D7 form.<br>(D7) | G7 form.<br>(E7) |
|---|---|---|---|---|---|---|---|---|
| 1 | 4 | 5 | 1 | 4 | 5 | 1 | 4 | 5 |
| D7 formation is the 1 chord | | | G7 formation is the 1 chord | | | A7 formation is the 1 chord | | |

22

The 4 chord is always two frets below the 5 chord, so you can play chord families like this:

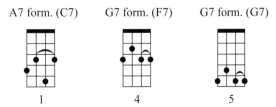

This 8-bar blues, played in two different keys, makes use of several chord families.

## BLUES AND TROUBLE—With Moveable Seventh Chords

TRACK 17

Words and Music by Fred Sokolow
Copyright © 2019 by HAL LEONARD LLC
International Copyright Secured   All Rights Reserved

Key of C:

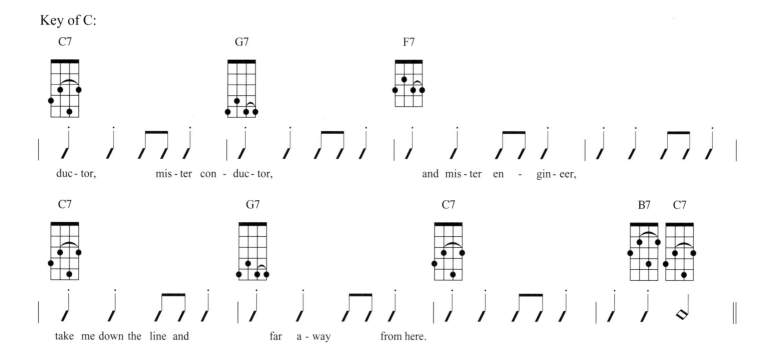

duc - tor,    mis - ter con - duc - tor,    and mis - ter en - gin - eer,

take me down the line and    far a - way    from here.

# THREE MOVEABLE MINOR CHORDS

The moveable major chord formations can be altered to create minor chords. Here they are:

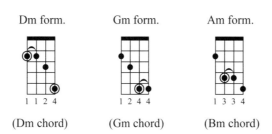

| Dm form. | Gm form. | Am form. |
|---|---|---|
| 1 1 2 4 | 1 2 4 4 | 1 3 3 4 |
| (Dm chord) | (Gm chord) | (Bm chord) |

## Minor Chord Families

Play them in their chord families:

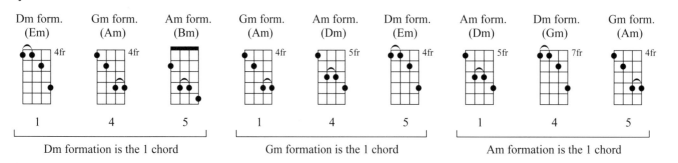

| Dm form. (Em) | Gm form. (Am) | Am form. (Bm) | Gm form. (Am) | Am form. (Dm) | Dm form. (Em) | Am form. (Dm) | Dm form. (Gm) | Gm form. (Am) |
|---|---|---|---|---|---|---|---|---|
| 4fr | 4fr | | 4fr | 5fr | 4fr | 5fr | 7fr | 4fr |
| 1 | 4 | 5 | 1 | 4 | 5 | 1 | 4 | 5 |

Dm formation is the 1 chord        Gm formation is the 1 chord        Am formation is the 1 chord

Play the following tune in three different keys, using all three minor chord families. The chord sequence is 1-, 4-, 5-, 1-. (The minus sign indicates a minor chord: 4- means "four minor.") Try moving it around the fretboard to get used to each chord family.

TRACK 18

## MINOR MELODY—With Moveable Minor Chords

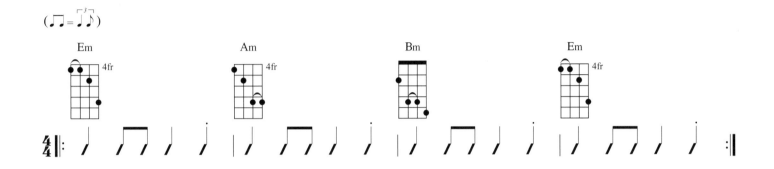

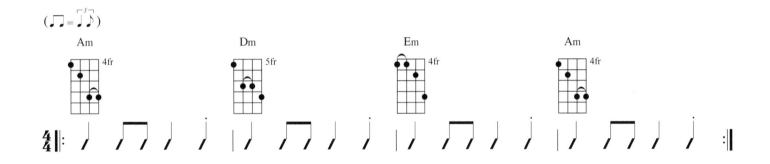

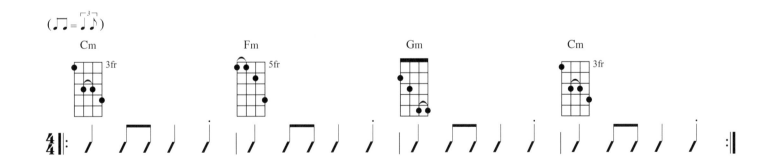

# JAZZ CHORDS

Dixieland, swing, jazz, and pop music make use of jazz chords like major sevenths, minor sixths, ninths, suspended chords, and augmented chords. These are just like the minor, major, and seventh chords you've already learned, only with a note added or altered, resulting in a subtler sound. Often, you can learn these chords by comparing them to the simpler major, minor, or seventh chords from which they're derived. In the comparisons below, the roots of the chords are circled.

Now make it a moveable shape by barring and moving it up a fret:

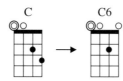

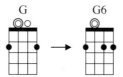

Here's the moveable version:

The "maj7" suffix means "major seventh."

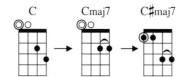 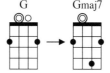

The plus sign (+) means "augmented."

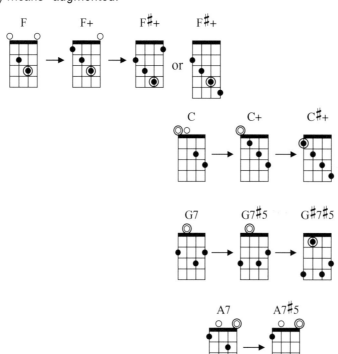

26

Here are some minor chord variations:

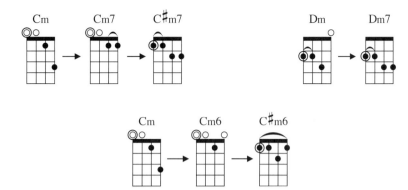

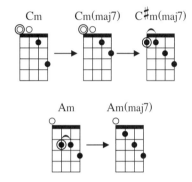

The "m(maj7)" suffix stands for "minor major seventh"—a very colorful chord indeed.

A ninth chord sounds like a seventh, only a little more sophisticated:

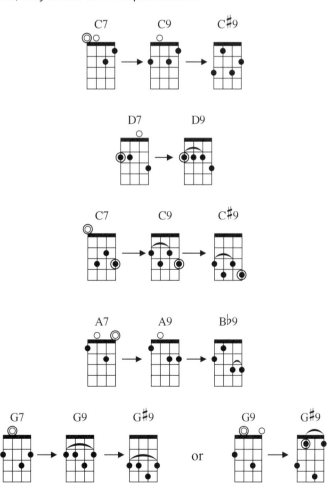

The "sus" suffix stands for "suspended."

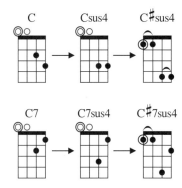

Adding a ♭9th to a dominant seventh chord makes it sound even tenser:

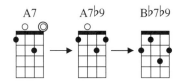

The degree symbol (°) means "diminished." The diminished seventh chord can be named by any of the four notes in the chord because it's *symmetrical*. This D°7 could also be called A♭°7, F°7, or B°7. Diminished chords repeat every four frets. These are all the same diminished chord:

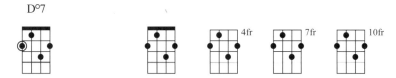

"The Sheik of Araby," a 1921 Tin Pan Alley hit, uses many of the above jazz chords. Silent film star Rudolph Valentino had a huge hit that year with the movie *The Sheik*, and the song exploited the popularity of that film. It became a jazz standard and is still performed by retro jazz and Dixieland bands. The Beatles performed it on their 1962 audition for Decca Records, but they didn't get the gig! This version is in the key of C.

TRACK 19

## THE SHEIK OF ARABY—Key of C

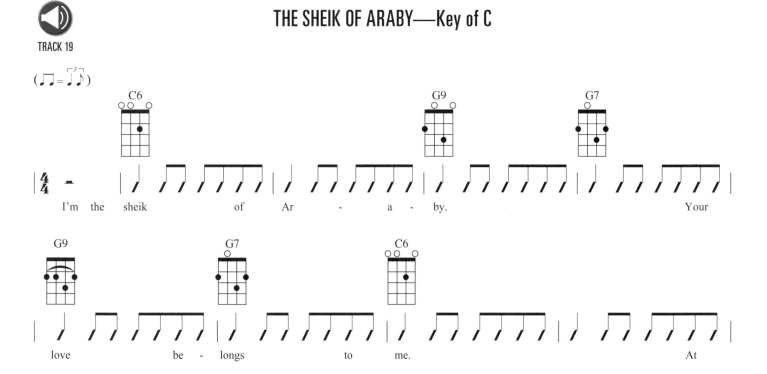

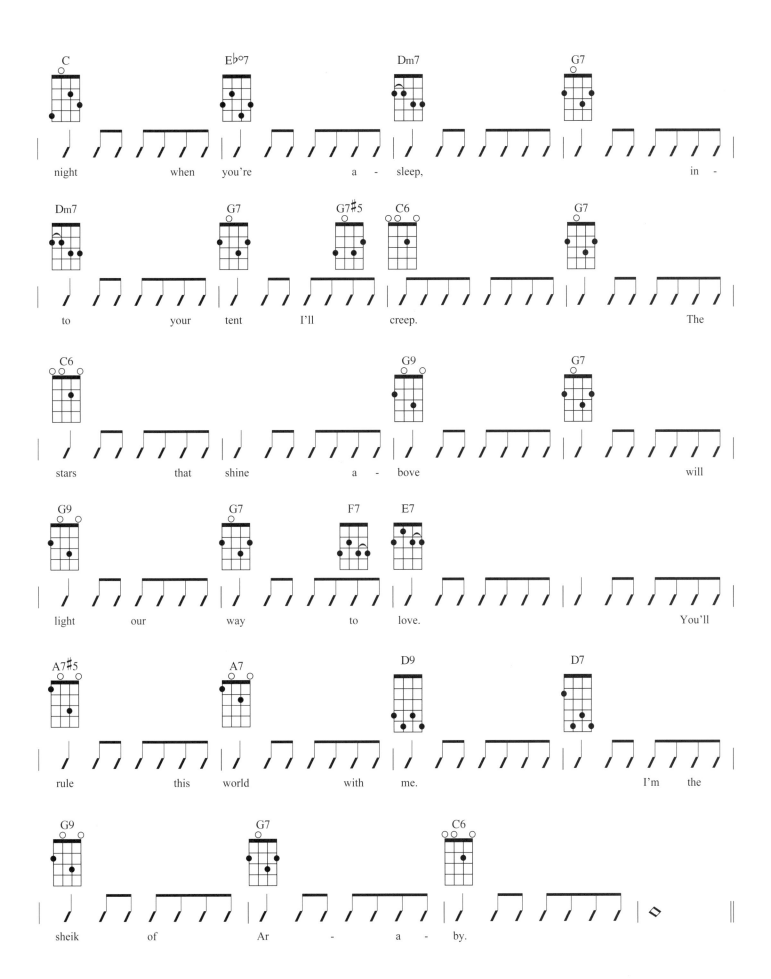

night        when you're      a - sleep,                                    in -

to          your        tent      I'll        creep.                              The

stars                   that      shine           a - bove                        will

light        our          way        to        love.                              You'll

rule                this        world        with        me.                       I'm the

sheik         of         Ar    -    a    -    by.

A classic tune from the "Great American Songbook," "When You're Smiling (The Whole World Smiles with You)" was a hit when Louis Armstrong recorded it in 1929 and has been recorded by countless jazz and pop singers since. This version is in the key of G.

## WHEN YOU'RE SMILING (THE WHOLE WORLD SMILES WITH YOU)—Key of G

TRACK 20

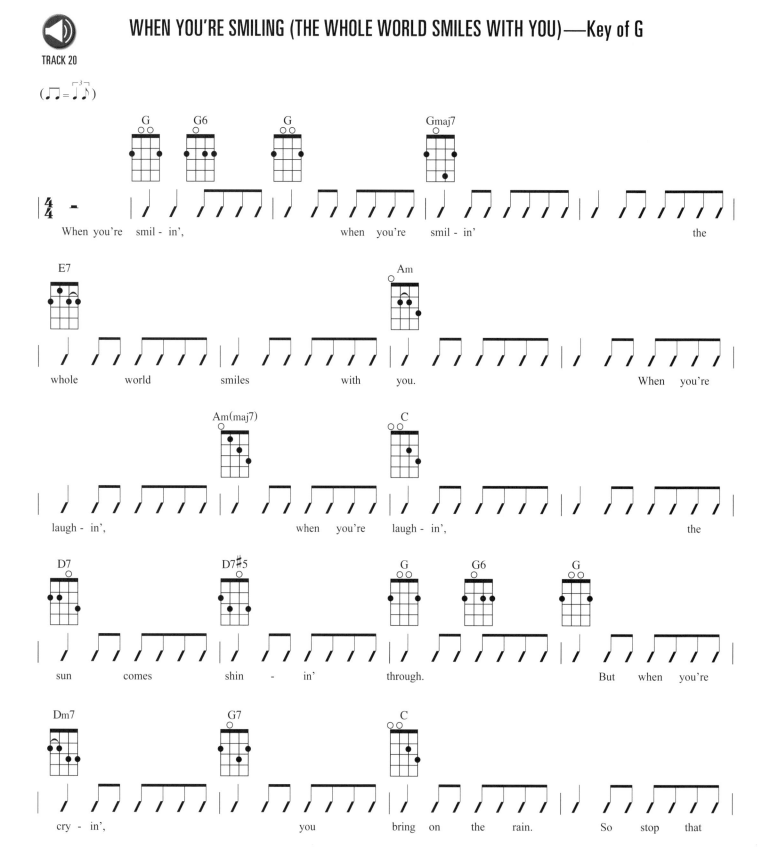

Words and Music by Mark Fisher, Joe Goodwin and Larry Shay
Copyright © 1928 EMI Mills Music Inc. and Music By Shay
Copyright Renewed
All Rights for EMI Mills Music Inc. Administered by EMI Mills Music Inc. (Publishing) and Alfred Music (Print)
All Rights for Music By Shay Administered by The Songwriters Guild Of America
International Copyright Secured All Rights Reserved

30

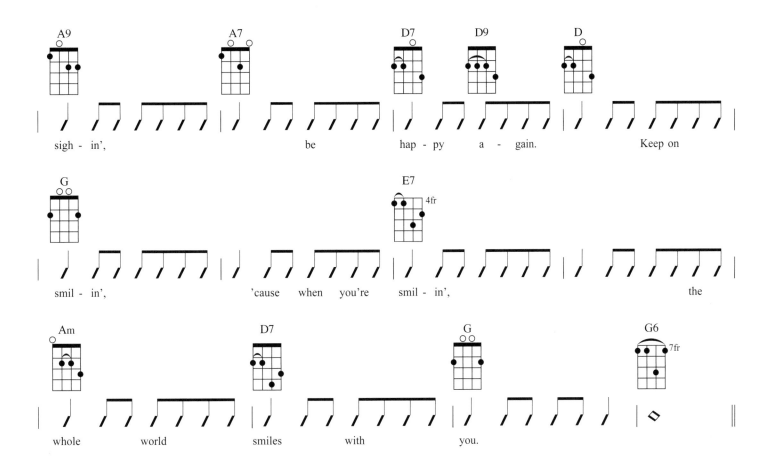

Louis Armstrong had a #1 pop hit with "Hello, Dolly!" in 1964, the year the Broadway show of the same name was produced. The song is in every Dixieland band's repertoire. This key of A version will help you practice moveable chord shapes.

**TRACK 21**

## HELLO, DOLLY!—Key of A

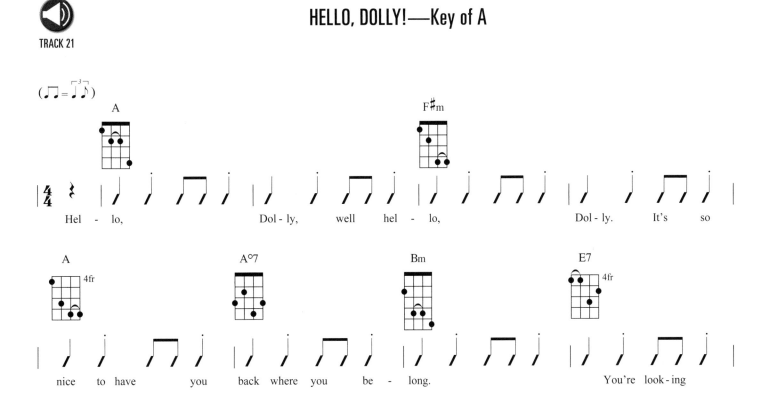

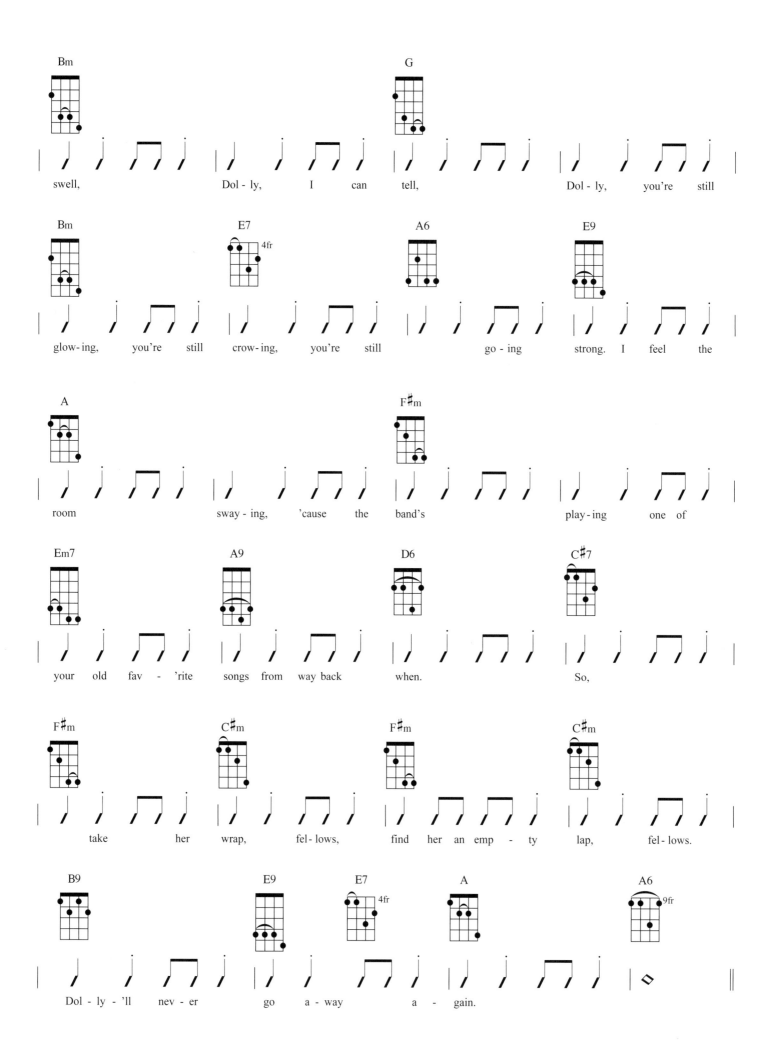

# SOLOING

## SINGLE-NOTE SOLOING WITH MAJOR SCALES

A soloist basically has three choices:

1. Play the melody

2. Embellish the melody

3. Freely improvise over the chord progression

Familiarity with major scales makes all three much easier to do, because: 1) so many songs have melodies that are based on the major scale, and 2) practicing and learning scales is one way to teach your fretting hand where the notes are on the banjo.

Practice each first-position major scale as written in a loop that goes up and down, over and over. Then play the song that follows. Once you've played the scale a number of times, try picking out simple melodies by ear. Pick songs you've known all your life, like "Yankee Doodle," "Twinkle, Twinkle Little Star," "Happy Birthday to You," and "This Land Is Your Land."

Each scale is written in music and tablature, along with a corresponding fretboard diagram. The numbers inside the circles indicate fingering: 1 = index finger, 2 = middle finger, 3 = ring finger, and 4 = little finger. The *roots* (the notes that name the scale) are double-circled.

## C MAJOR SCALE

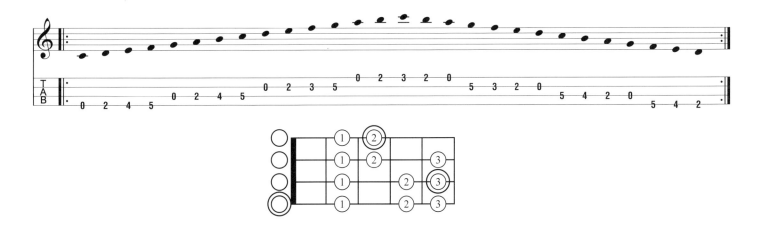

Here's "Little Brown Jug" in two different octaves. The second time around, there are strums filling out the melodic pauses. That means you have to be playing the right chord at the right time, while picking out the melody.

TRACK 22

## LITTLE BROWN JUG—Key of C

# F MAJOR SCALE

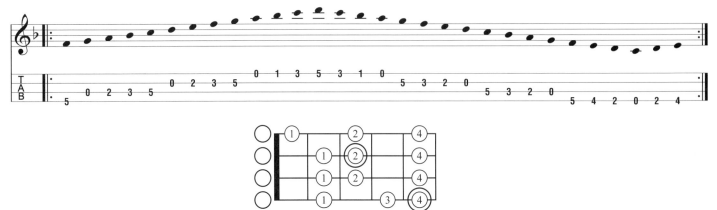

The first version of "When the Saints Go Marching In" is just the melody. Chord strums are added the second time around, and the melody is played an octave higher.

TRACK 23

## WHEN THE SAINTS GO MARCHING IN—Key of F

"Midnight in Moscow" is a Dixieland standard. This version is in the key of D minor, which uses the same scale as F major. The melody is played on the lower strings, with occasional fill-in strums on the higher strings.

TRACK 24

## MIDNIGHT IN MOSCOW—Key of D Minor

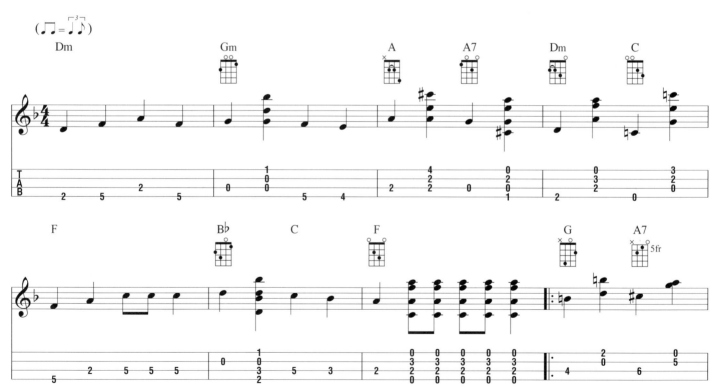

Based on a song by Vassili Soloviev-Sedoy and M. Matusovsky
New Music by Kenny Ball
© Copyright 1961 (Renewed) Tyler Music Ltd., London, England
TRO - Melody Trails, Inc., New York, controls all publication rights for the U.S.A. and Canada
International Copyright Secured
All Rights Reserved Including Public Performance For Profit
Used by Permission

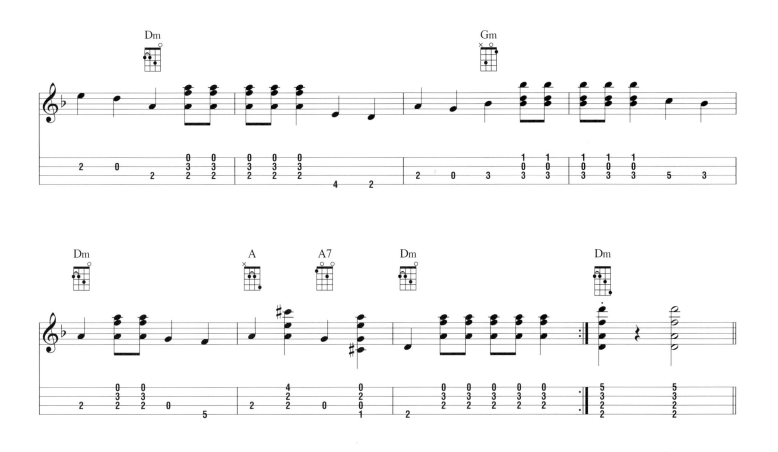

## G MAJOR SCALE

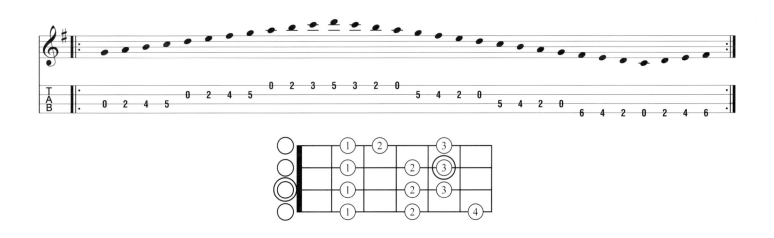

## Tremolo

*Tremolo*, the rapid down-and-up picking that is so characteristic of tenor banjo, comes from the wrist. Your arm should barely move, and your wrist should be loose. You can use tremolo on a chord or, as in "Careless Love" below, on single notes. In music and tablature, tremolo is indicated with the ⚡ symbol.

The first time around "Careless Love," below, chords are strummed when there are sustained melody notes. The second time, an octave higher, the tremolo technique makes certain notes sustain.

TRACK 25

## CARELESS LOVE—Key of G

## D MAJOR SCALE

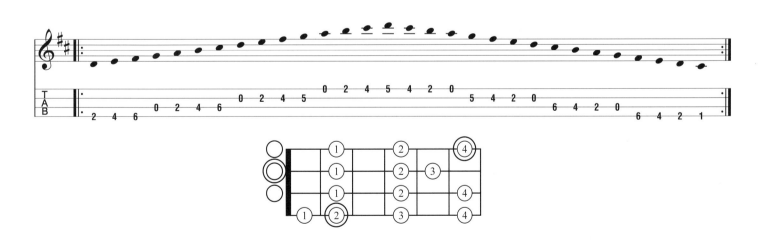

The following version of "Down by the Riverside" fills out the melody with chord strumming.

TRACK 26

## DOWN BY THE RIVERSIDE—Key of D

# A MAJOR SCALE

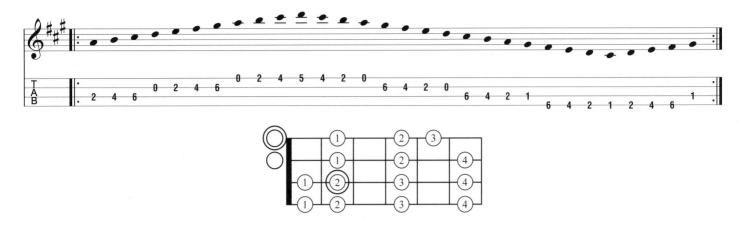

Practice the A major scale and then play this version of "Frankie and Johnny." It consists of the melody with some strums for fills.

**TRACK 27**

## FRANKIE AND JOHNNY—Key of A

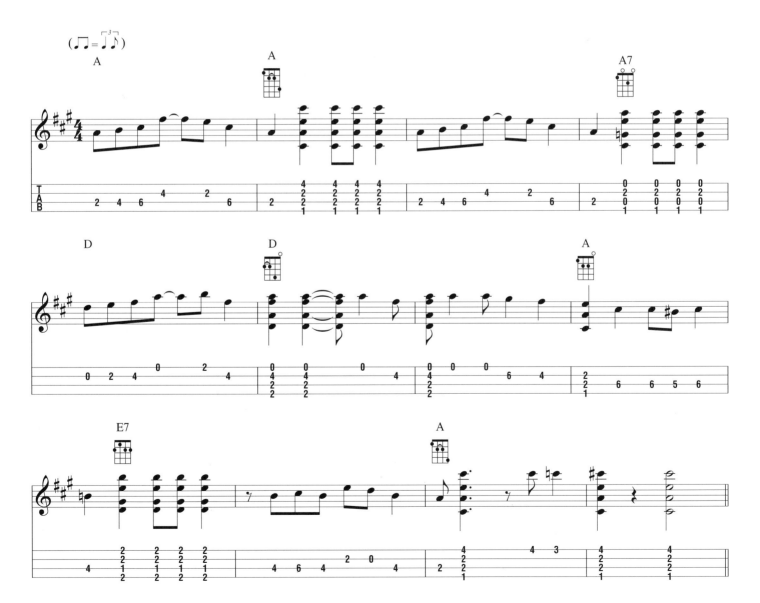

# B♭ MAJOR SCALE

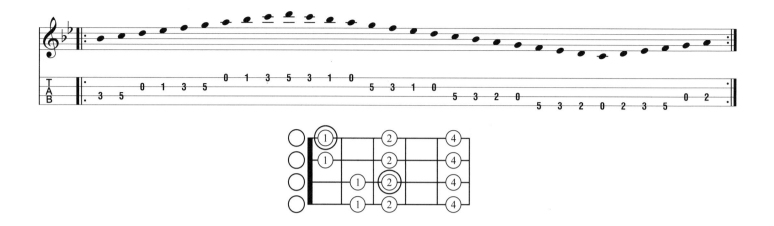

Once you've practiced the B♭ major scale, play this version of "Little Brown Jug."

## LITTLE BROWN JUG—Key of B♭

TRACK 28

# IMPROVISING WITH FIRST-POSITION MAJOR SCALES

Some improvising involves embellishing a melody and adding notes and fills. Another way to improvise is to disregard the melody entirely and make up licks and phrases that fit the chord progression. This is essentially spontaneous composition, and it's done in all genres (jazz, blues, rock, country, etc.). In both cases, most of your ad-lib licks can come from the major scale of a song's key.

Here's a solo to "When the Saints Go Marching In" that features both types of improvisation. Play it first and then try to make up your own variations using similar phrasing.

TRACK 29

### WHEN THE SAINTS GO MARCHING IN—Ad-Lib Solo in F

## Adding Blue Notes

"Blue notes" are flatted 3rds, flatted 7ths, and flatted 5ths—none of which are in the major scale. Sprinkle them into your major scale-based improvisation to create a bluesy effect. The following ad-lib solo to "Frankie and Johnny" in C is based on the C major scale but includes several blue notes.

Here are some blue notes in the key of C:

TRACK 30

# FRANKIE AND JOHNNY—Ad-Lib Solo in C with Blue Notes

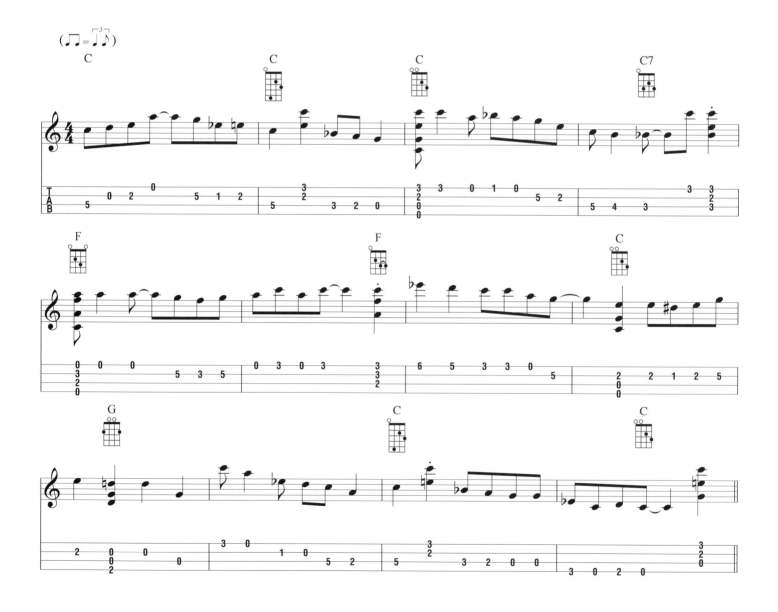

Here's a bluesy ad-lib solo to "Beale Street Blues" in G. First, look at the key of G blue notes:

## BEALE STREET BLUES—Ad-Lib Solo in G with Blue Notes

# MOVEABLE MAJOR SCALES

This section covers three moveable major scales. Each is based on one of the three moveable major chords shown in the "Accompaniment" section. Each one is moveable; you can play the same pattern all over the fretboard in different keys. The root note of each scale is circled in the fretboard diagrams. The fingering is indicated by numbers in the circles. Practice each scale as it's written in the music/tab, going up and down, over and over, until your fingers start to feel the pattern. Then play the tunes that follow.

The three old fiddle tunes that follow are usually played using easy, first-position scales that include as many open strings as possible. These up-the-neck arrangements make good exercises for the moveable major scales. Like most fiddle tunes, these three have two repeated sections: an A part and a B part. When you play AABB, you've gone around the tune once.

## D Formation-Based Moveable Major Scale

Here's a D major scale that's loosely based on the D formation major chord. You don't have to fret the D formation to play the scale. Instead, your fretting hand hovers around the chord shape and uses it as a frame of reference to place the scale where you want it. It's in the key of D as written below, but if you move it up two frets, it's an E major scale.

- Be sure to use the fingering that's indicated by the circled numbers in the fretboard diagram.
- When playing the scale as written in the music/tab, be sure to start with your index finger on the fourth string/second fret.
- Practice the scale in other keys as well. Move it up two frets for an E major scale, etc.

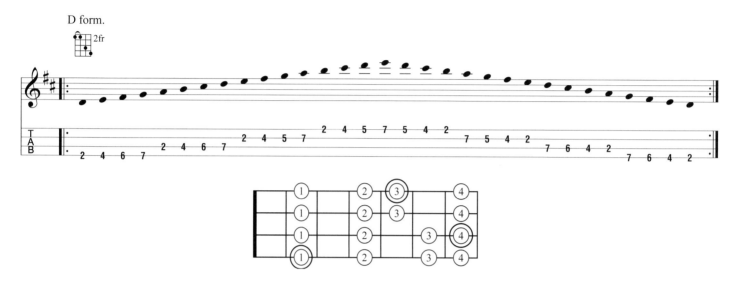

"Devil's Dream" is an old Scottish fiddle tune usually played in the key of A. This version makes use of the D formation-based moveable major scale, moved up seven frets higher, so it's in the key of A. You'll see the direction "8va throughout" stated at the start of the tune. *8va* means that the music sounds one octave higher than the written notation. This keeps the notes on the staff and easier to read.

TRACK 32

# DEVIL'S DREAM—Key of A

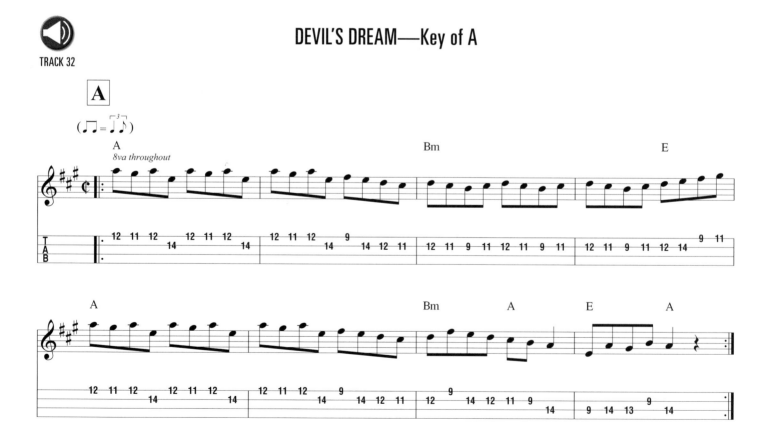

Traditional
Copyright © 2019 by HAL LEONARD LLC
International Copyright Secured   All Rights Reserved

46

**B**

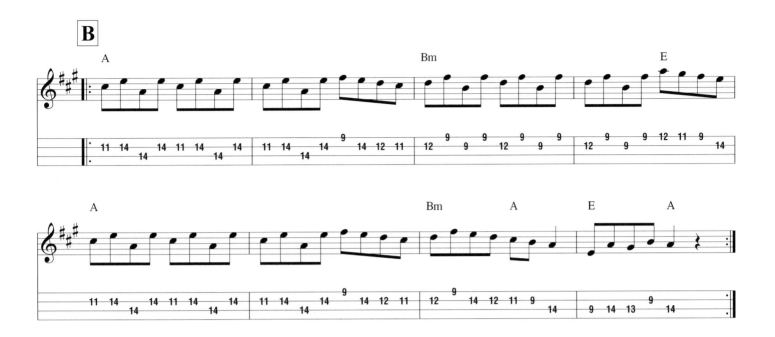

## A Formation-Based Moveable Major Scale

This is a D major scale, but it can be played higher up the neck in any key. Be sure to start the scale with your ring finger on the third string/seventh fret. Then play the scale pattern in higher keys further up the neck.

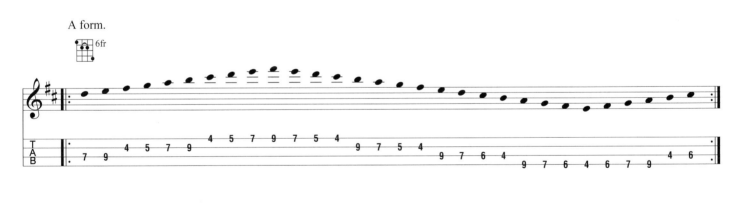

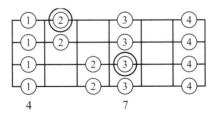

This version of "The Irish Washerwoman" is played in its traditional key of G using the A formation-based moveable major scale. That's the D major scale you just played, moved up five frets.

## THE IRISH WASHERWOMAN—Key of G

Irish Folksong
Copyright © 2019 by HAL LEONARD LLC
International Copyright Secured   All Rights Reserved

## G Formation-Based Moveable Major Scale

This scale pattern starts with the little finger on the fourth string/14th fret. It's a D major scale.

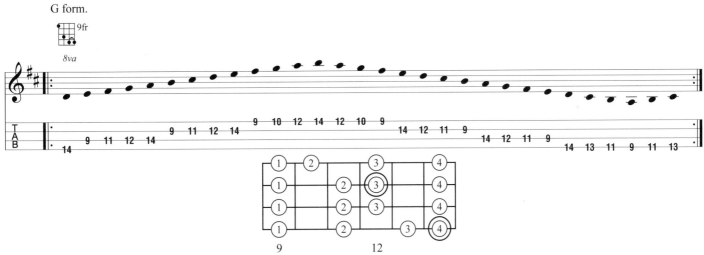

"Whiskey Before Breakfast" is a Canadian tune that's usually played in the key of D. This version is also in D, using the G formation-based moveable scale, as written above.

**TRACK 34**

# WHISKEY BEFORE BREAKFAST—Key of D

# CHORD-MELODY PLAYING

So far, you've played melodic, single-note solos "filled out" with some chord strumming. However, swing and Dixieland banjoists play more chord solos than single-note solos. The following tracks illustrate the *chord-melody style*; they include more chords and less single notes. If you learn them, you'll begin to understand how to create your own chord-melody solos. Here are a few tips:

- **Where to Place the Melody:** The melody of the song stands out clearly when you make the melody note the highest note of each chord. Whenever possible, play the melody on the first string and support it with a chord. If the melody note is on the second string, strum the fourth, third, and second strings only—don't play the first string. The following solos—all standards in the Dixieland repertoire—illustrate this technique.

- **Finding Different Voicings of a Chord:** It helps to know several ways to voice any chord. Since melodies go up high and come down low, you need a high, medium, and low voicing for every chord you come across. The following charts show how to find different voicings of major, minor, and seventh chords. The patterns shown in these charts are moveable. For example, the D formation D chord reaches from the second fret to the fifth fret, and the next voicing of the D chord (the A formation D chord) starts at the sixth fret. *Wherever you play the D formation, the next voicing of that chord is the A formation one fret higher.*

**Major Chord Voicings (These are all D chords)**

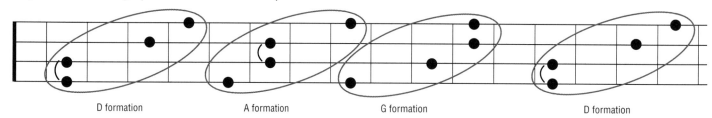

D formation      A formation      G formation      D formation

**Seventh Chord Voicings (These are all D7 chords)**

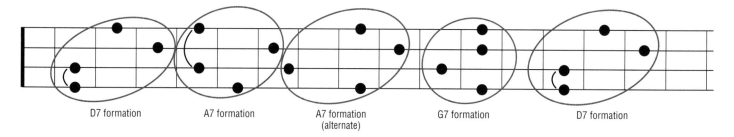

D7 formation    A7 formation    A7 formation (alternate)    G7 formation    D7 formation

**Minor Chord Voicings (These are all D minor chords)**

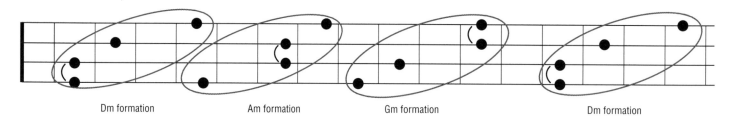

Dm formation      Am formation      Gm formation      Dm formation

In the "Accompaniment" section, under the heading "Jazz Chords," you learned how to turn many major, minor, or seventh chords into subtler jazz chords by changing one note. It's easier to remember a new chord shape if you see how it resembles a chord you already know. In the following chart, you can see how a D formation major chord becomes a D6 or Dmaj7 shape just by changing one note. There are similar charts for the A and G formations.

# CHORD TYPES AND CHORD INTERVALS

There are basically three types of chords: major, minor, and seventh chords. All the subtler chords (ninths, minor sixths, etc.) are one of these three types with an extra added note or two. To better understand how you're altering the major chords that are written in the following large grids, first look at the intervals of each chord type.

The numbers represent intervals in the major scale. For example, a major chord is 1–3–5, so C major is C–E–G: the first, third, and fifth notes in the C major scale.

The eighth note is the same as the first note in a major scale, but it's an octave higher. The ninth is the same as a second, and the 13th is the same as a sixth.

| | |
|---|---|
| **major:** 1–3–5 | **7♯5:** 1–3–♯5–♭7 |
| **6:** 1–3–5–6 | **9:** 1–3–5–♭7–9 |
| **maj7 (major seven):** 1–3–5–7 | **13:** 1–3–5–♭7–9–13 |
| **+ (augmented):** 1–3–♯5 | **m (minor):** 1–♭3–5 |
| **add 9:** 1–3–5–9 | **m6:** 1–♭3–5–6 |
| **7:** 1–3–5–♭7 | **m7:** 1–♭3–5–♭7 |

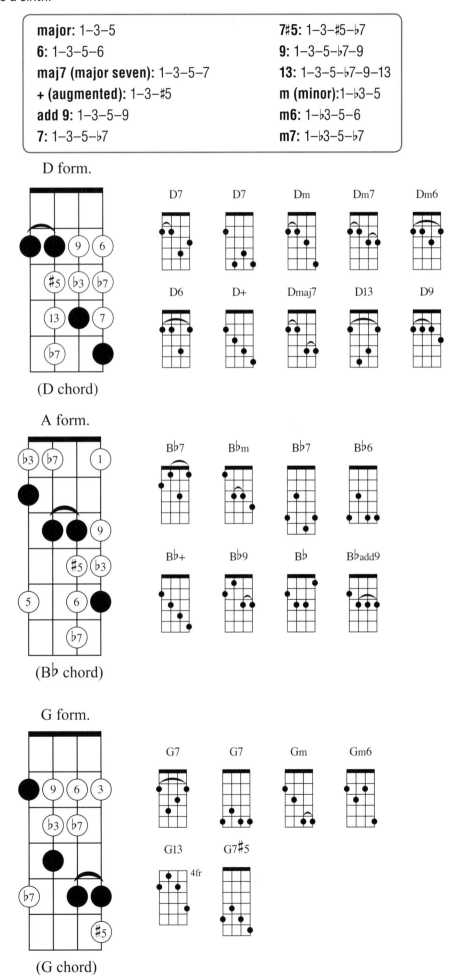

D form.

(D chord)

A form.

(B♭ chord)

G form.

(G chord)

Before learning to play the chord-melody arrangement of "Yes Sir, That's My Baby," study the song's chord shapes and listen to the recording. Do this with each of the following eleven songs. They're all standards in the Dixieland and retro jazz repertoires.

TRACK 35

## YES SIR, THAT'S MY BABY—Key of G

# FIVE FOOT TWO, EYES OF BLUE (HAS ANYBODY SEEN MY GIRL?)—Key of C

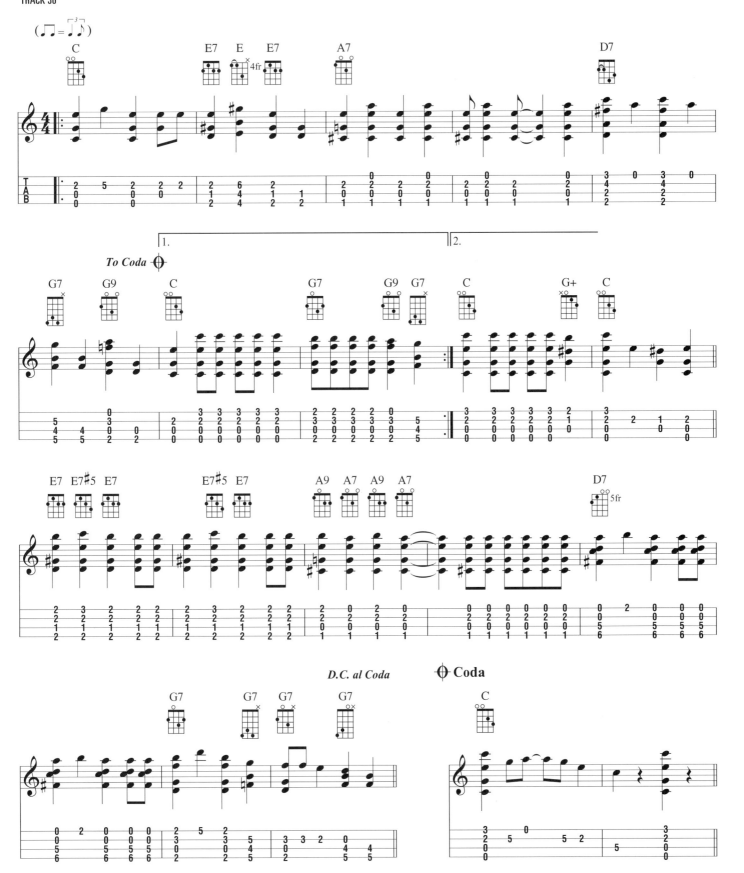

Words by Joe Young and Sam Lewis
Music by Ray Henderson
© 1925 LEO FEIST, INC.
© Renewed 1953 WAROCK CORP., EMI FEIST CATALOG INC. and RAY HENDERSON MUSIC CO. in the United States
All Rights for EMI FEIST CATALOG INC. Administered by EMI FEIST CATALOG INC. (Publishing) and ALFRED MUSIC (Print)
All Rights for the Sam Lewis and Ray Henderson shares in the British Reversionary Territories Administered by REDWOOD MUSIC LTD.
All Rights Reserved

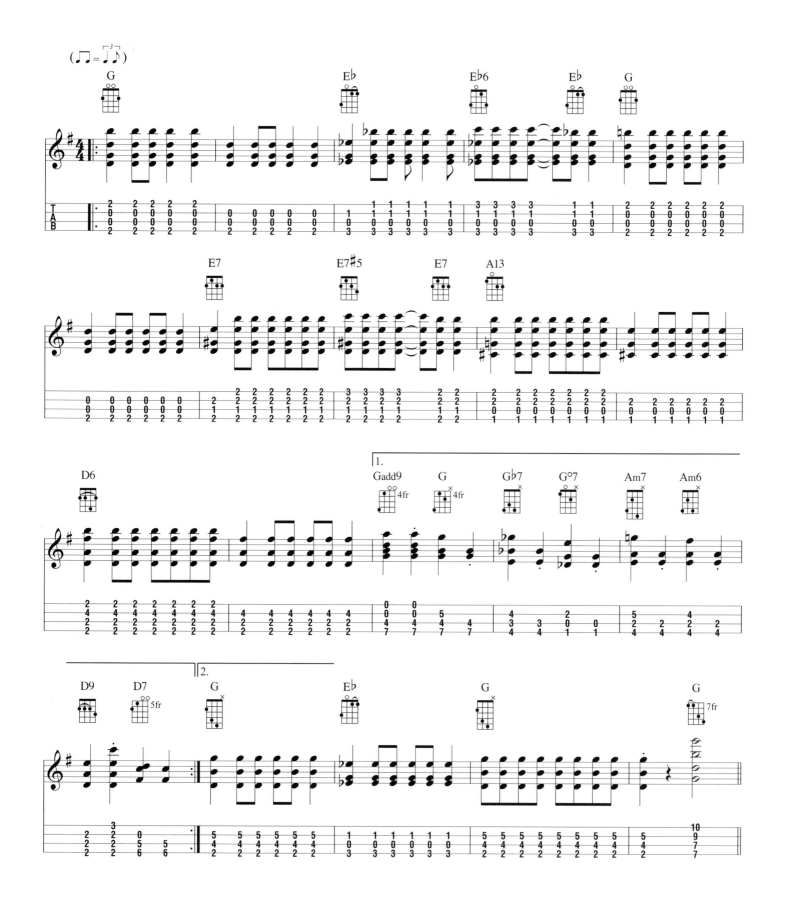

Words and Music by Fred Hamm, Dave Bennett, Bert Lown and Chauncey Gray
Copyright © 1930 by Bourne Co. (ASCAP)
Copyright Renewed
International Copyright Secured  All Rights Reserved

# WHEN YOU'RE SMILING (THE WHOLE WORLD SMILES WITH YOU)—Key of C

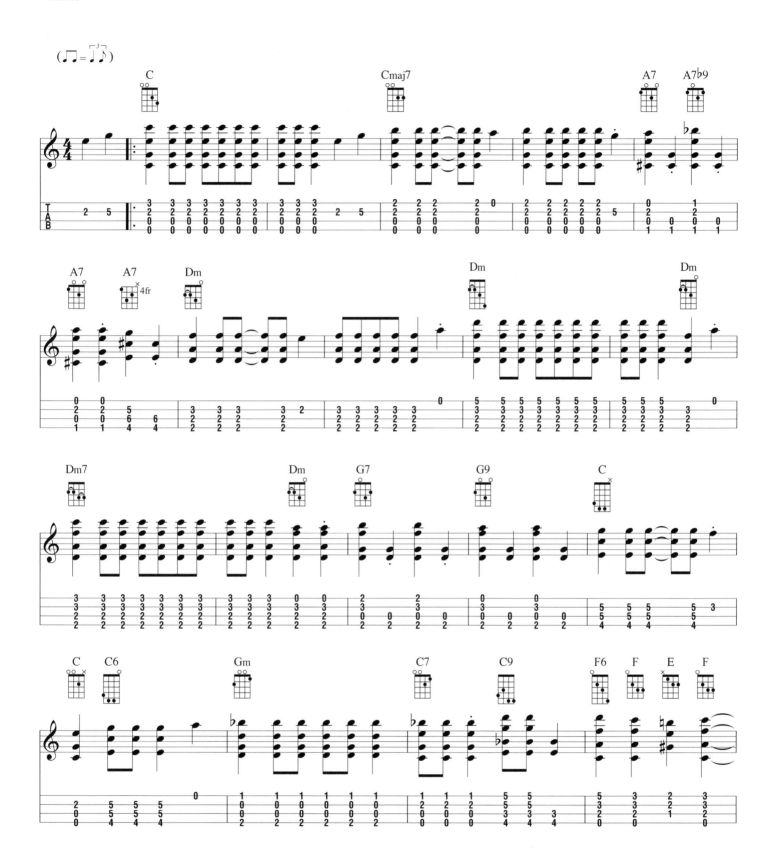

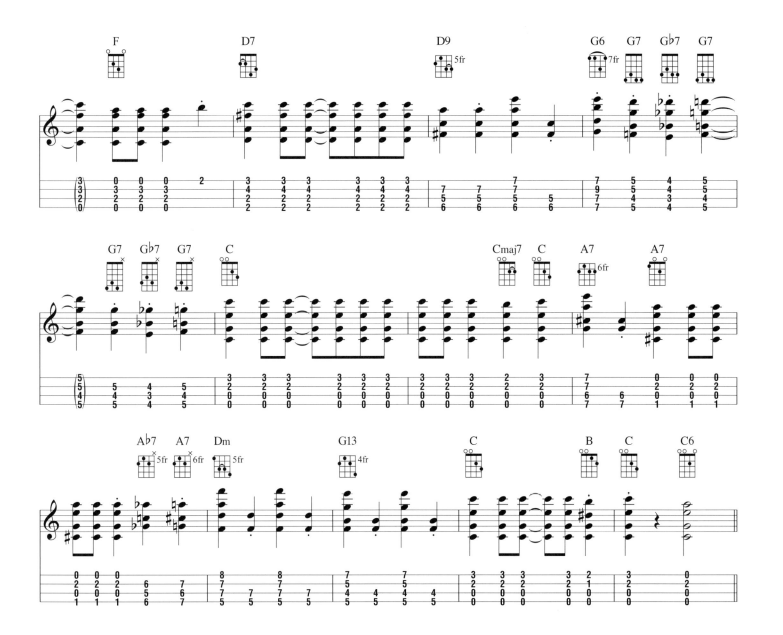

TRACK 39

## SWEET GEORGIA BROWN—Key of F

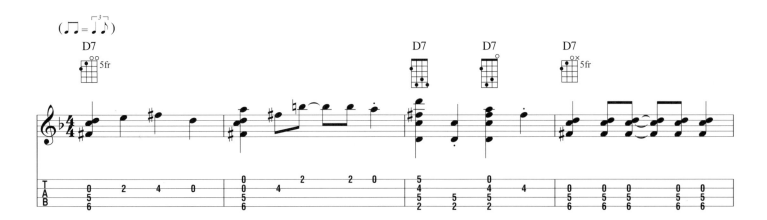

# THE SHEIK OF ARABY—Key of B♭

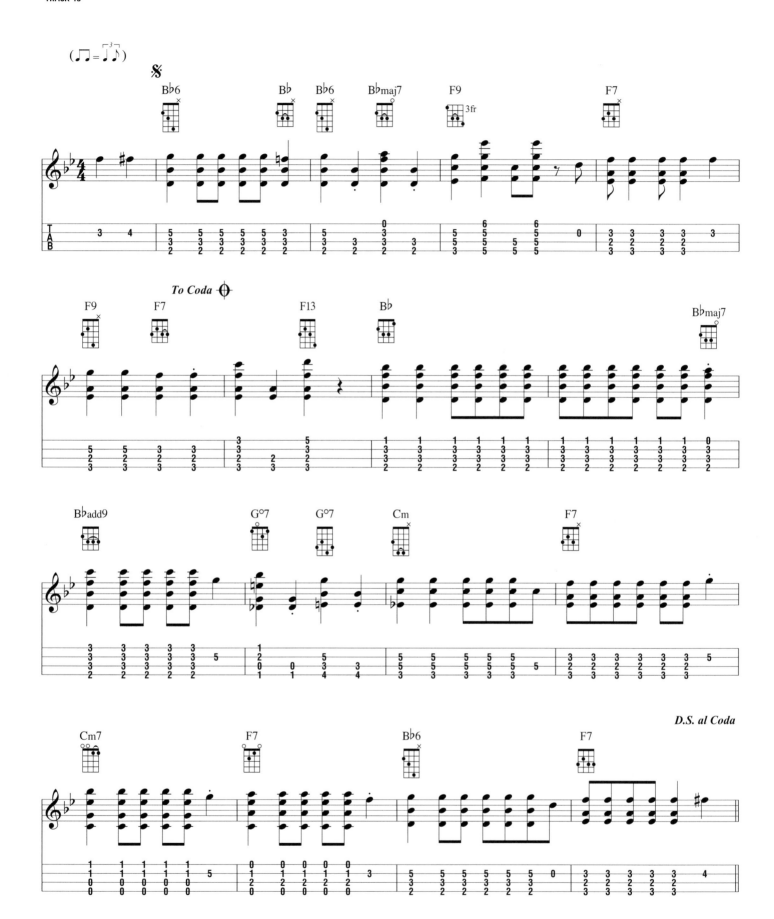

Words by Harry B. Smith and Francis Wheeler
Music by Ted Snyder
Copyright © 2019 by HAL LEONARD LLC
International Copyright Secured   All Rights Reserved

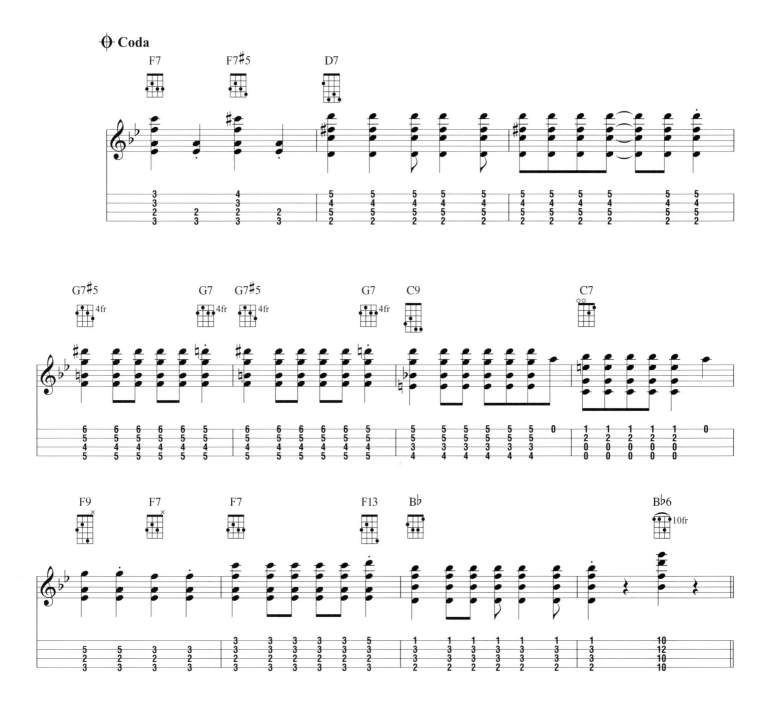

# BABY FACE—Key of B♭

Words and Music by Benny Davis and Harry Akst
Copyright © 1926 (Renewed) B & G AKST PUBLISHING CO. and BENNY DAVIS MUSIC
All Rights for B & G AKST PUBLISHING CO. Administered by THE SONGWRITERS GUILD OF AMERICA
Harry Akst Reversionary Interest Controlled by BOURNE CO. (ASCAP)
International Copyright Secured  All Rights Reserved

# I'VE FOUND A NEW BABY—Key of D Minor

# WHO'S SORRY NOW—Key of B♭

from THREE LITTLE WORDS
Words by Bert Kalmar and Harry Ruby
Music by Ted Snyder

## ⊕ Coda

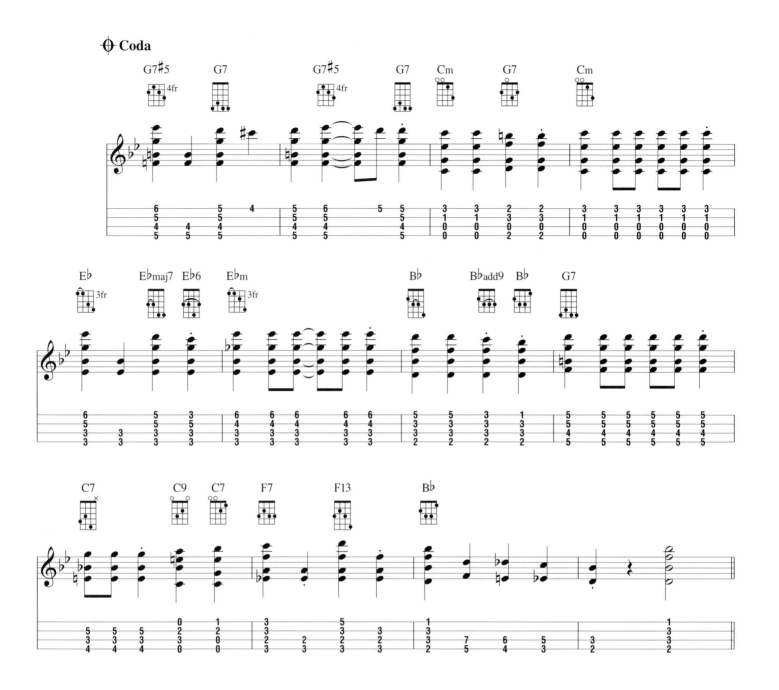

TRACK 44

Words by Jack Yellen
Music by Milton Ager
© 1927 WARNER BROS. INC.

# SOMEBODY STOLE MY GAL—Key of E♭

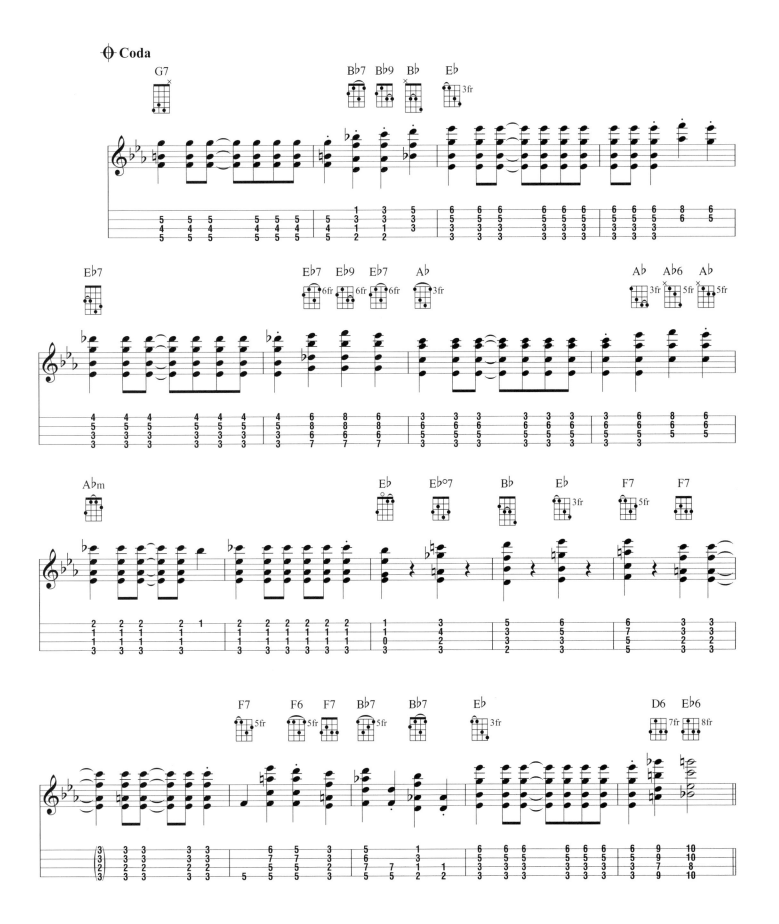

# CONVERSION TO IRISH TENOR BANJO

## TUNING AND NOTES ON THE FRETBOARD

Most Irish tenor banjoists tune five frets lower than the standard tuning, which results in G–D–A–E. This is the same as a violin or mandolin, only an octave lower. You may want to use heavier strings for this tuning.

Here's the string-to-string tuning method:

- Tune the G, fourth string to a tuning fork, piano, or other source.

- Fret the G string at the seventh fret. Match the D, third string to this note.

- Fret the D string at the seventh fret. Match the A, second string to this note.

- Fret the A string at the seventh fret. Match the E, first string to this note.

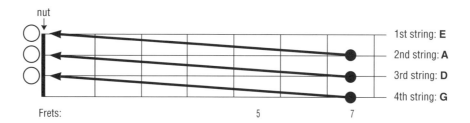

Or you can use the tuning notes on this audio track:

 **Tuning Notes**

TRACK 46

Here are the notes on the fretboard with this tuning:

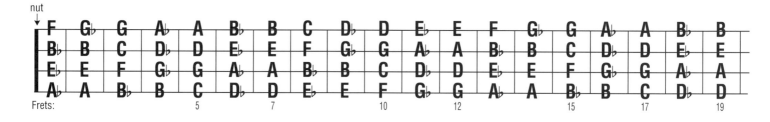

You can use all your standard-tuning chord shapes and scales with this tuning, but the names of chords and notes will be a 5th higher. In other words, your C chord is now called G, your G chord is a D chord, and so on.

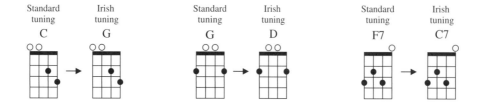

Frequently, the banjoist in an Irish band plays the song's melody in unison with several other instruments. Here are the three fiddle tunes you played earlier using moveable major scales. They're in the same traditional keys as before, but this time they're set in first position, which makes them much easier to play! Since "Devil's Dream" is in the key of A, you can use the first-position D major scale you learned for standard tuning.

TRACK 47

## DEVIL'S DREAM—Key of A

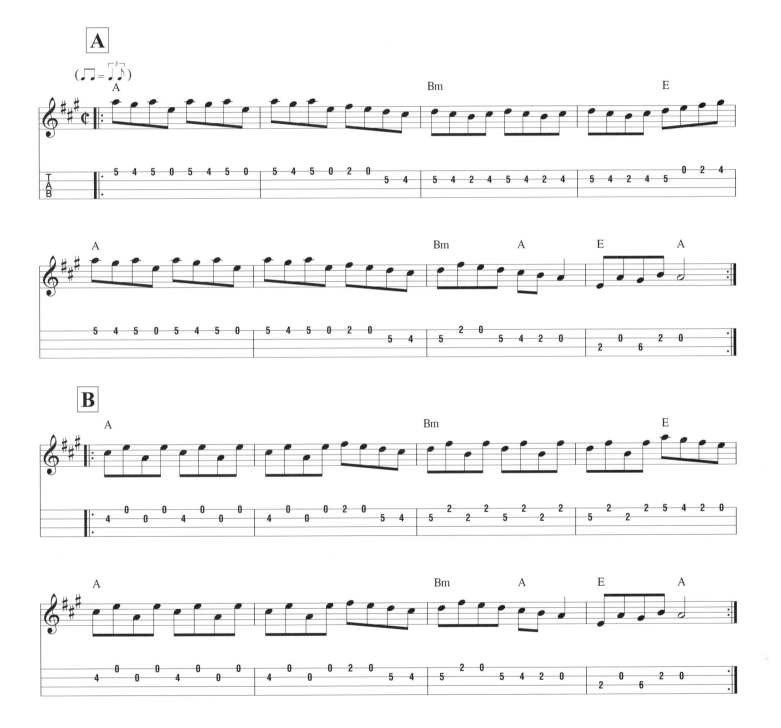

"The Irish Washerwoman" is in the key of G, so use your standard tuning/first-position D major scale.

TRACK 48

## THE IRISH WASHERWOMAN—Key of G

Irish Folksong
Copyright © 2019 by HAL LEONARD LLC
International Copyright Secured   All Rights Reserved

"Whiskey Before Breakfast" is in the key of D, so use your standard tuning/first-position A major scale.

## WHISKEY BEFORE BREAKFAST—Key of D

TRACK 49

# CHICAGO TUNING

Some tenor banjoists, especially jazz players, use the Chicago tuning: D–G–B–E. Since this is the same as the top four strings of the guitar, it enables guitarists to play tenor banjo without learning a new set of chords and scales. Baritone ukulele is also tuned this way. For extensive instruction on this tuning, see the Hal Leonard book *Fretboard Roadmaps for Baritone Ukulele* by Fred Sokolow.

# ABOUT THE AUTHOR

Fred Sokolow is best-known as the author of over 150 instructional and transcription books and DVDs for guitar, mandolin, banjo, ukulele, Dobro, and lap steel. Fred has long been a well-known West Coast, multi-string performer and recording artist, particularly on the acoustic music scene. He is often featured as a performer and teacher at ukulele, banjo, and guitar festivals all over the world. The diverse musical genres covered in his books and DVDs, along with several bluegrass, jazz, and rock CDs he has released, demonstrate his mastery of many musical styles. Whether he's playing Delta bottleneck blues, bluegrass, traditional Hawaiian uke, old-time or Dixieland banjo, 1930s swing guitar, or screaming rock solos, he does it with authenticity and passion.

Fred's other Hal Leonard banjo books include:
*Fretboard Roadmaps – 5-String Banjo,* book/audio
*The Complete Bluegrass Banjo Method,* book/audio
*The Beatles for Banjo*, book
*101 5-String Banjo Tips*, book/CD
*Blues Banjo*, book/audio

Email Fred with any questions about this or his other books at: **Sokolowmusic.com**.